HOW TO BUILD CONFIDENCE IN KIDS

Proven Strategies to Build Resilience, Self-Esteem, Foster Confidence and Success in Today's Competitive World

ALINA ROBERTSON

Disclaimer

The information provided in this book is for educational and informational purposes only and is not intended as a substitute for professional medical advice, diagnosis, or treatment. Always seek the advice of your physician or other qualified healthcare provider with any questions you may have regarding a medical condition. The author and publisher of this book are not responsible for any adverse effects or consequences resulting from the use of the information presented herein. Readers assume full responsibility for their own actions and decisions.

TABLE OF CONTENTS

Introduction

The journey of parenting and caregiving, one of the most profound gifts we can offer children is the development of confidence. "How to Build Confidence in Kids" is your guide to understanding and cultivating this essential quality in the young minds entrusted to your care.

Understanding the Importance of Confidence in Children

Confidence is the cornerstone upon which children build their futures. It is more than mere self-assurance; it is the bedrock of self-belief that empowers them to navigate life's challenges with resilience and determination. Here's why confidence is crucial for children:

1. **Academic Excellence:** Confident children approach learning with enthusiasm and curiosity. They willingly embrace new ideas, ask questions, and

engage actively in the learning process, leading to academic success and a lifelong love of learning.

2. **Social Flourishing:** Confidence enables children to form meaningful connections with their peers, communicate effectively, and navigate social interactions with ease. They assert themselves, express thoughts and feelings, and forge positive relationships built on mutual respect and understanding.

3. **Embracing Challenges:** Confident children see challenges as opportunities for growth and learning. They exhibit resilience, perseverance, and a willingness to try again, even when faced with setbacks or failures.

4. **Goal Pursuit**: With confidence as their foundation, children are emboldened to set ambitious goals and work diligently towards achieving them.

They possess the self-belief and determination necessary to overcome obstacles and turn their dreams into reality.

5. **Positive Self-Image:** Confidence fosters a positive self-image and a strong sense of self-worth in children. They recognize and appreciate their unique strengths and talents, celebrate accomplishments, and approach life with optimism and self-assurance.

Understanding the importance of confidence lays the groundwork for effectively supporting children in their journey of self-discovery and growth.

Understanding Confidence

Confidence is a powerful attribute that influences nearly every aspect of a child's life. It shapes their beliefs, attitudes, and behaviors, ultimately impacting their academic success, social interactions, and overall well-being. In this section, we will explore what confidence truly means and why children need to develop it.

Defining Confidence and Its Components

Confidence is often described as a belief in oneself and one's abilities. It is the inner conviction that you can achieve your goals and overcome obstacles. However, confidence is not a static trait; it is dynamic and can vary in different situations and contexts.

Confidence comprises several components, each contributing to a child's overall sense of self-assurance:

1. **Self-Efficacy:** This refers to a child's belief in their ability to accomplish specific tasks or goals. When children have high self-efficacy, they feel competent in tackling challenges, leading to increased motivation and performance.

2. **Self-Image:** Self-image encompasses how children perceive themselves and their worth. A positive self-image involves accepting oneself, recognizing one's strengths and weaknesses, and feeling comfortable in one's skin.

3. **Self-Esteem:** Self-esteem relates to a child's overall evaluation of their worth and value as a person. It reflects their sense of self-worth and plays a crucial role in shaping their confidence levels.

4. **Self-Confidence:** Self-confidence is the belief in one's ability to succeed in various situations. It involves trust in oneself, a willingness to take risks, and the resilience to bounce back from setbacks.

When these components align harmoniously, children develop a robust sense of confidence that empowers them to navigate life's challenges with courage and resilience. However, it is essential to recognize that confidence is not a fixed trait and can fluctuate over time. External factors, such as experiences, feedback from others, and environmental influences, can all impact a child's confidence levels.

The Benefits of Building Confidence in Kids

Building confidence in children yields a myriad of benefits that extend far beyond their immediate circumstances.

Here are some of the key advantages of fostering confidence in young minds:

1. **Improved Academic Performance:** Confident children approach learning with enthusiasm and curiosity. They actively engage in classroom activities, participate in discussions, and take academic risks. As a result, they often excel academically and develop a lifelong love of learning.

2. **Enhanced Social Skills:** Confidence empowers children to navigate social interactions with ease and grace. Confident children are more likely to initiate conversations, assert themselves in group settings, and forge positive relationships with their peers. They exhibit empathy, kindness, and respect towards others, fostering a supportive and inclusive social environment.

3. **Greater Resilience:** Confidence equips children with the resilience

needed to overcome obstacles and setbacks. Confident children view challenges as opportunities for growth and learning rather than insurmountable barriers. They bounce back from failure with determination and optimism, emerging stronger and more resilient than before.

4. **Increased Independence:** Confidence encourages independence and autonomy in children. Confident children trust their abilities and judgment, allowing them to make decisions and take initiative in various aspects of their lives. They are more likely to pursue their interests, explore new opportunities, and chart their path towards success.

5. **Positive Self-Image:** Confidence fosters a positive self-image and a strong sense of self-worth in children. Confident children recognize and appreciate their unique qualities, talents,

and contributions. They embrace their individuality and celebrate their accomplishments, cultivating a healthy sense of self-esteem and self-acceptance.

By nurturing confidence in children, we empower them to fulfill their potential and thrive in all aspects of their lives. As caregivers and educators, we play a vital role in instilling confidence in the children entrusted to our care. Through encouragement, support, and positive reinforcement, we can help children develop the self-belief and resilience needed to overcome challenges and pursue their dreams with confidence and determination.

Identifying Challenges to Confidence

As children navigate the journey of growing up, they encounter various obstacles that can hinder the development of confidence. Understanding these challenges is crucial for parents, educators, and caregivers, as it allows them to provide targeted support and guidance to help children overcome these hurdles. In this section, we will explore common obstacles faced by children and external factors that impact confidence development.

Common Obstacles Faced by Children

1. **Fear of Failure:** Fear of failure is a pervasive challenge that can significantly impact a child's confidence. Children may avoid trying new things or taking risks out of fear of not

succeeding. This fear can stem from pressure to perform well academically, socially, or in extracurricular activities.

2. **Comparison to Peers:** In today's competitive society, children are often subjected to comparisons with their peers. Whether it's academic achievements, athletic abilities, or social popularity, children may feel inadequate when they perceive themselves as falling short compared to others. This constant comparison can erode their confidence and self-esteem over time.

3. **Negative Self-Talk:** Children are not immune to negative self-talk, internalizing critical or disparaging remarks made by others or themselves. Negative self-talk can undermine their confidence and lead to feelings of self-doubt and worthlessness. It is essential to help children recognize and challenge these negative thoughts, replacing them

with positive affirmations and self-encouragement.

4. **Perfectionism:** Some children may struggle with perfectionism, setting impossibly high standards for themselves and becoming overly critical when they fail to meet them. Perfectionism can create a vicious cycle of self-doubt and anxiety, preventing children from taking risks or trying new things for fear of not being perfect.

5. **Bullying and Peer Pressure:** Bullying and peer pressure can have a devastating impact on a child's confidence and self-esteem. Children who experience bullying may internalize negative messages about themselves, leading to feelings of shame, isolation, and inadequacy. Similarly, peer pressure to conform to certain behaviors or standards can undermine a child's sense of self and authenticity.

6. **Lack of Supportive Environment:** A lack of support from parents, caregivers, or educators can also hinder confidence development in children. When children do not feel valued, respected, or encouraged in their environment, they may struggle to believe in themselves and their abilities.

External Factors Impacting Confidence Development

1. **Parental Influence:** Parents play a significant role in shaping their children's confidence levels. Positive parental involvement, encouragement, and support can bolster a child's self-belief and resilience. Conversely, overly critical or demanding parenting styles can undermine confidence and contribute to feelings of inadequacy.

2. **Educational Environment:** The school environment plays a crucial role in shaping children's confidence and self-esteem. Supportive teachers,

positive peer relationships, and opportunities for success can boost confidence levels, while a lack of support or a negative school climate can erode confidence and motivation.

3. **Media and Society:** Media portrayals and societal expectations can impact children's perceptions of themselves and their worth. Unrealistic beauty standards, gender stereotypes, and portrayals of success can shape children's beliefs about what it means to be confident and successful.

4. **Community and Cultural Influences:** Cultural norms, traditions, and community values can influence children's confidence in profound ways. Children from marginalized or underrepresented communities may face unique challenges related to identity, belonging, and acceptance, impacting their confidence and self-esteem.

5. **Traumatic Experiences:** Children who experience trauma or adverse childhood experiences may struggle with confidence issues stemming from feelings of insecurity, fear, or shame. It is essential to provide trauma-informed support and resources to help these children heal and rebuild their confidence.

Identifying and addressing these challenges and external factors is essential for supporting children in developing confidence and resilience. By creating a supportive and nurturing environment, offering encouragement and validation, and teaching coping skills and self-compassion, we can empower children to overcome obstacles and thrive with confidence.

Building a Foundation for Confidence

As a parent, caregiver, or educator, you have the power to lay the groundwork for your child's confidence and self-belief. Building a strong foundation for confidence begins with creating a supportive environment at home and nurturing your child's self-esteem and positive self-image. In this section, we will explore practical strategies and techniques to help you foster confidence in the children under your care.

Creating a Supportive Environment at Home

1. **Unconditional Love and Acceptance:** Show your child unconditional love and acceptance, regardless of their achievements or shortcomings. Let them know that they are valued and loved for who they are, not just for what they do.

2. **Encouragement and Positive Reinforcement:** Encourage your child's efforts and accomplishments, no matter how big or small. Offer specific praise and positive reinforcement to build their confidence and self-esteem.

3. **Open Communication:** Create an environment where open communication is encouraged and valued. Listen to your child's thoughts, feelings, and concerns without judgment and offer support and guidance when needed.

4. **Setting Realistic Expectations:** Avoid placing unrealistic expectations or pressure on your child to excel in every aspect of their life. Instead, focus on setting realistic goals and celebrating their progress and achievements along the way.

5. **Modeling Confidence:** Be a positive role model for your child by demonstrating confidence and self-assurance in your actions and behaviors. Show them that it's okay to make mistakes, learn from them, and encourage them to do the same.

6. **Creating a Safe and Supportive Space:** Foster a safe and supportive home environment where your child feels comfortable expressing themselves and taking risks. Encourage them to explore their interests and passions without fear of judgment or criticism.

Nurturing Self-Esteem and Positive Self-Image

1. **Promoting Self-Discovery:** Encourage your child to explore their interests, talents, and passions to help them discover their strengths and build confidence in their abilities.

2. **Celebrating Individuality:** Celebrate your child's unique qualities, talents, and achievements, and encourage them to embrace their individuality. Help them recognize and appreciate the things that make them special.

3. **Offering Constructive Feedback:** Provide constructive feedback to help your child learn and grow, but be mindful of how you deliver it. Focus on highlighting their strengths and offering guidance for improvement in a supportive and encouraging manner.

4. **Encouraging Positive Self-Talk**: Teach your child to use positive self-talk and affirmations to combat negative thoughts and build confidence. Encourage them to replace self-doubt with self-encouragement and remind them of their capabilities.

5. **Teaching Coping Skills:** Equip your child with coping skills and strategies to

help them navigate challenges and setbacks. Teach them how to problem-solve, cope with stress, and bounce back from failure with resilience and determination.

6. **Cultivating Gratitude and Mindfulness:** Foster a sense of gratitude and mindfulness in your child by encouraging them to focus on the present moment and appreciate the blessings in their life. Help them cultivate a positive outlook and resilience in the face of adversity.

By creating a supportive environment at home and nurturing your child's self-esteem and positive self-image, you are laying the foundation for their confidence and success in life. Your love, encouragement, and guidance will empower them to navigate life's challenges with resilience, optimism, and unwavering self-belief.

Effective Communication Techniques

Effective communication is key to building strong, positive relationships with children and fostering their confidence and self-esteem. By communicating effectively, you can create a supportive and nurturing environment where children feel valued, heard, and understood. In this section, we will explore practical techniques for communicating positively with children and encouraging openness and expressiveness.

Communicating Positively with Children

1. **Use Positive Language:** Choose words and phrases that are positive and uplifting when speaking to children. Avoid using negative language or criticism, as this can undermine their confidence and self-esteem. Instead,

focus on highlighting their strengths and offering encouragement and praise for their efforts and accomplishments.

2. **Active Listening:** Practice active listening when communicating with children, which involves giving them your full attention, maintaining eye contact, and showing genuine interest in what they have to say. Listen without interrupting, and validate their feelings and experiences to make them feel heard and understood.

3. **Be Empathetic:** Show empathy and understanding towards children's thoughts, feelings, and experiences. Put yourself in their shoes and try to see things from their perspective. Acknowledge their emotions and validate their experiences, even if you don't necessarily agree with them.

4. **Provide Constructive Feedback:** When offering feedback or guidance,

focus on providing constructive criticism that is specific, actionable, and encouraging. Avoid harsh criticism or negative judgment, as this can be demoralizing and undermine confidence. Instead, offer suggestions for improvement and praise their efforts and progress.

5. **Encourage Independence:** Empower children to express themselves and make their own decisions by encouraging independence and autonomy. Offer guidance and support when needed, but allow them the freedom to explore their interests, make choices, and learn from their experiences.

6. **Be Approachable:** Create an environment where children feel comfortable approaching you with their thoughts, concerns, and questions. Be approachable and open-minded, and encourage open communication by

being receptive to their ideas and opinions.

Encouraging Openness and Expressiveness

1. **Create a Safe Space:** Foster an environment where children feel safe and secure expressing themselves without fear of judgment or criticism. Create open lines of communication and let them know that they can come to you with anything, no matter how big or small.

2. **Validate Feelings:** Validate children's feelings and emotions by acknowledging and accepting them without judgment. Let them know that it's okay to feel a range of emotions and that you are there to support them through whatever they may be experiencing.

3. **Encourage Self-Expression:** Encourage children to express themselves creatively through art,

writing, music, or other forms of self-expression. Provide opportunities for them to explore their interests and passions and express themselves in meaningful ways.

4. **Model Openness:** Be a role model for openness and expressiveness by sharing your thoughts, feelings, and experiences with your children in a respectful and age-appropriate manner. Demonstrate healthy communication skills and encourage them to do the same.

5. **Active Engagement:** Actively engage with children in conversations and activities that promote openness and expressiveness. Ask open-ended questions, actively listen to their responses, and engage in meaningful discussions that encourage them to share their thoughts and feelings.

6. **Respect Boundaries:** Respect children's boundaries and personal space, and avoid pressuring them to share more than they are comfortable with. Let them know that they can set boundaries and that their privacy will be respected.

By communicating positively with children and encouraging openness and expressiveness, you create a supportive and nurturing environment where they feel valued, heard, and understood. Your efforts to foster healthy communication skills will empower children to express themselves confidently and develop strong, positive relationships with others.

Encouraging Independence and Resilience

Encouraging independence and resilience in children is essential for their overall growth and development. By fostering independence in decision-making and teaching coping skills and resilience, you empower children to navigate life's challenges with confidence and adaptability. In this section, we will explore practical strategies to promote independence and resilience in the children under your care.

Fostering Independence in Decision-Making

1. **Offer Choices:** Give children opportunities to make decisions and choices in their daily lives. Offer them a range of options and allow them to select their preferences. This could be as simple as choosing what to wear,

what to eat for breakfast, or what activity to do after school.

2.   **Encourage   Problem-Solving:** Encourage children to solve problems and overcome obstacles independently. Instead of immediately stepping in to offer solutions, ask open-ended questions that prompt them to think critically and come up with their solutions. This helps build their problem-solving skills and confidence in their abilities.

3. **Provide Guidance and Support:** While it's important to encourage independence, provide guidance and support when needed. Offer assistance and advice when children are facing challenges or making difficult decisions, but empower them to ultimately make their own choices.

4. **Celebrate Successes:** Celebrate children's successes and

accomplishments, no matter how small. Acknowledge their efforts and praise their decision-making skills, reinforcing their confidence and sense of autonomy.

5. **Allow for Mistakes:** Encourage children to embrace failure as a natural part of the learning process. Help them understand that making mistakes is okay and that it's an opportunity to learn and grow. Encourage a growth mindset by emphasizing the importance of perseverance and resilience in the face of setbacks.

6. **Gradually Increase Responsibility:** Gradually increase children's responsibilities and independence as they grow older and demonstrate readiness. Give them age-appropriate tasks and chores to complete independently, such as tidying their room, preparing their snacks, or managing their homework.

Teaching Coping Skills and Resilience

1. **Emotional Regulation:** Teach children healthy ways to manage their emotions and cope with stress. Encourage them to practice deep breathing, mindfulness, or other relaxation techniques when they're feeling overwhelmed or anxious. Help them identify and label their emotions, and validate their feelings without judgment.

2. **Problem-Solving Skills:** Teach children effective problem-solving skills to help them navigate challenges and setbacks. Encourage them to break problems down into manageable steps, brainstorm possible solutions, and evaluate the consequences of each option. Empower them to take action and implement their chosen solution.

3. **Encourage Flexibility:** Foster flexibility and adaptability in children by helping them understand that life is full of unexpected twists and turns. Encourage them to approach new situations with an open mind and a willingness to adapt to changing circumstances.

4. **Build a Support Network:** Help children cultivate strong social connections and supportive relationships with family, friends, teachers, and other trusted adults. Encourage open communication and provide opportunities for children to seek help and support when needed.

5. **Positive Self-Talk:** Teach children to cultivate a positive inner dialogue and challenge negative thoughts and beliefs. Encourage them to replace self-doubt with self-compassion and optimism, reminding them of their strengths and abilities.

6. **Model Resilience:** Be a positive role model for resilience by demonstrating healthy coping skills and perseverance in the face of adversity. Share your own experiences of overcoming challenges and setbacks, and highlight the importance of resilience in achieving success.

By encouraging independence in decision-making and teaching coping skills and resilience, you equip children with the tools and confidence they need to navigate life's challenges with resilience and adaptability. Your guidance and support play a vital role in helping children develop the skills and mindset necessary to thrive in an ever-changing world.

Promoting Growth Mindset and Goal Setting

Encouraging a growth mindset and goal setting in children is crucial for their academic and personal development. By instilling a growth mindset and teaching them how to set and achieve realistic goals, you empower children to embrace challenges, persist in the face of setbacks, and reach their full potential. In this section, we will explore practical strategies to promote a growth mindset and goal-setting in the children under your care.

Instilling a Growth Mindset in Children

1. **Emphasize Effort and Persistence:** Teach children that success is not solely determined by innate talent or intelligence but by effort and persistence. Encourage them to embrace challenges as opportunities for

growth and learning, rather than avoiding them out of fear of failure.

2. **Praise Process Over Outcome:** Focus on praising children's efforts, strategies, and progress rather than solely on their achievements. Highlight their hard work, perseverance, and resilience, reinforcing the idea that success comes from continuous effort and improvement.

3. **Normalize Mistakes and Failure:** Help children understand that making mistakes and experiencing failure are natural and essential parts of the learning process. Encourage them to view setbacks as opportunities to learn, grow, and improve, rather than as indicators of their intelligence or worth.

4. **Encourage a Love of Learning:** Foster a love of learning in children by encouraging curiosity, exploration, and intellectual curiosity. Provide

opportunities for them to pursue their interests, ask questions, and engage in hands-on learning experiences that ignite their passion for learning.

5. **Teach the Power of Yet:** Introduce children to the concept of "yet," emphasizing that they may not have mastered a particular skill or concept yet, but with effort and perseverance, they can improve and achieve their goals over time.

6. **Model a Growth Mindset:** Be a positive role model for a growth mindset by demonstrating resilience, perseverance, and a willingness to learn and grow. Share stories of your challenges, setbacks, and successes, and highlight the importance of maintaining a positive attitude and growth mindset in overcoming obstacles.

Setting and Achieving Realistic Goals

1. **SMART Goals:** Teach children how to set SMART goals—specific, measurable, achievable, relevant, and time-bound. Help them identify specific goals they want to achieve and break them down into smaller, manageable steps.

2. **Encourage Ownership:** Encourage children to take ownership of their goals by involving them in the goal-setting process. Help them identify their strengths, interests, and areas for improvement, and support them in setting goals that align with their aspirations and values.

3. **Provide Support and Guidance:** Offer support and guidance to help children develop action plans and strategies for achieving their goals. Break down large goals into smaller, achievable tasks, and provide

resources, encouragement, and accountability along the way.

4. **Celebrate Progress:** Celebrate children's progress and achievements as they work towards their goals. Acknowledge their efforts and milestones, and praise their dedication, perseverance, and resilience in overcoming obstacles and staying focused on their objectives.

5. **Adjust and Adapt:** Encourage children to be flexible and adaptable in their goal-setting process. Help them recognize when adjustments may be necessary and encourage them to revise their goals or action plans as needed based on changing circumstances or new information.

6. **Reflect and Learn:** Encourage children to reflect on their progress and experiences as they work towards their goals. Help them identify what went

well, what challenges they faced, and what they learned from the process. Encourage self-reflection and self-awareness to foster continuous growth and improvement.

By promoting a growth mindset and goal setting in children, you empower them to take ownership of their learning and personal development. Your guidance and support play a crucial role in helping children develop the skills, attitudes, and habits necessary to set meaningful goals, overcome obstacles, and achieve success in all areas of their lives.

Embracing Failure and Learning from Mistakes

Embracing failure and learning from mistakes are essential components of personal growth and development. As a caregiver or educator, it's important to teach children that failure is not something to be feared or avoided, but rather embraced as a natural and necessary part of the learning process. In this section, we will explore practical strategies to normalize failure as part of learning and encourage reflection and adaptation in children.

Normalizing Failure as Part of Learning

1. **Reframe Failure as Feedback:** Help children understand that failure is not a reflection of their worth or intelligence but rather feedback that can help them learn and grow. Encourage them to view setbacks as opportunities to identify

areas for improvement and develop resilience and perseverance.

2. **Share Personal Stories:** Share stories of your own experiences with failure and how you learned and grew from them. By normalizing failure and demonstrating that everyone experiences setbacks at times, you help children feel less alone in their struggles and more empowered to persevere in the face of adversity.

3. **Celebrate Effort and Progress:** Shift the focus from outcomes to effort and progress by celebrating children's hard work, perseverance, and resilience, regardless of the outcome. Recognize their willingness to take risks, try new things, and learn from their mistakes, reinforcing the idea that effort and growth are more important than perfection.

4. **Encourage Risk-Taking:** Create a supportive environment where children feel comfortable taking risks and trying new things. Encourage them to step outside their comfort zone, challenge themselves, and pursue their passions, knowing that failure is a natural part of the learning process.

5. **Provide Constructive Feedback:** Offer constructive feedback that focuses on specific areas for improvement and provides guidance for future success. Help children identify what went wrong, what they learned from the experience, and how they can apply that knowledge to future endeavors.

6. **Encourage Resilience:** Teach children resilience by helping them develop coping skills and strategies to bounce back from failure. Encourage them to stay positive, maintain a growth mindset, and persevere in the face of setbacks, knowing that they can

overcome challenges and succeed in the long run.

Encouraging Reflection and Adaptation

1. **Promote Self-Reflection:** Encourage children to reflect on their experiences and identify what they did well, what they could improve upon, and what they learned from the situation. Provide prompts or journaling exercises to help them process their thoughts and emotions and gain insights into their strengths and areas for growth.

2. **Set Aside Time for Reflection:** Create dedicated time and space for reflection and self-assessment in children's daily routines. This could be done through regular check-ins or reflection activities at the end of the day or week, allowing children to pause, reflect, and set intentions for future growth.

3. **Encourage Adaptation:** Teach children the importance of adapting to changing circumstances and learning from their experiences. Help them identify alternative strategies or approaches when faced with obstacles or setbacks and encourage them to be flexible and open-minded in their problem-solving.

4. **Highlight Learning Opportunities:** Help children see failure as an opportunity for learning and growth rather than a roadblock to success. Highlight the valuable lessons they can glean from their experiences and encourage them to apply that knowledge to future situations, fostering a continuous cycle of learning and improvement.

5. **Model Reflective Behavior:** Be a positive role model for reflection and adaptation by openly sharing your own experiences of learning and growth.

Demonstrate how you reflect on your successes and failures, adjust your approach when necessary, and continue to strive for improvement over time.

6. **Provide Supportive Guidance:** Offer guidance and support as children navigate the process of reflection and adaptation. Be patient and empathetic as they grapple with their emotions and insights, and provide encouragement and reassurance that failure is a natural part of the learning journey.

By normalizing failure as part of learning and encouraging reflection and adaptation, you help children develop the resilience, perseverance, and growth mindset needed to thrive in an ever-changing world. Your support and guidance play a crucial role in helping children embrace failure as an opportunity for growth and develop the skills and mindset necessary to overcome obstacles and achieve success in all areas of their lives.

Encouraging Healthy Risk-Taking and Exploration

As a caregiver or educator, fostering healthy risk-taking and exploration is essential for children's development. By striking a balance between safety and opportunities for growth and encouraging curiosity and exploration, you empower children to expand their horizons, build confidence, and develop critical skills for success. In this section, we will explore practical strategies to promote healthy risk-taking and exploration in children.

Balancing Safety with Opportunities for Growth

1. **Establish Clear Boundaries:** Set clear boundaries and guidelines to ensure children's safety while still allowing for exploration and risk-taking within those boundaries. Clearly communicate rules and expectations,

and provide supervision and guidance as needed to help children navigate new experiences safely.

2. **Assess Risks:** Assess the level of risk involved in different activities and environments and take appropriate precautions to mitigate potential hazards. Consider factors such as age, developmental stage, and individual abilities when determining the level of supervision and support needed.

3. **Encourage Calculated Risks:** Encourage children to take calculated risks that offer opportunities for growth and learning while still ensuring their safety. Help them assess the potential risks and benefits of different activities and make informed decisions about whether to proceed.

4. **Provide Supportive Guidance:** Offer supportive guidance and encouragement as children navigate

new experiences and challenges. Be available to answer questions, provide reassurance, and offer assistance as needed, while still allowing children to take ownership of their decisions and actions.

5. **Model Risk-Taking Behavior:** Be a positive role model for healthy risk-taking by demonstrating a willingness to try new things, take on challenges, and step outside your comfort zone. Share stories of your own experiences with risk-taking and exploration, highlighting the valuable lessons you learned along the way.

6. **Celebrate Efforts and Progress:** Celebrate children's efforts and progress as they engage in healthy risk-taking and exploration, regardless of the outcome. Focus on the process rather than the outcome, and praise their courage, curiosity, and willingness to step outside their comfort zone.

Encouraging Curiosity and Exploration

1. **Create a Stimulating Environment:** Create an environment that stimulates children's curiosity and encourages exploration. Provide a variety of materials, resources, and opportunities for hands-on learning and discovery, and allow children to follow their interests and pursue their passions.

2. **Ask Open-Ended Questions:** Encourage children to ask questions, explore ideas, and seek answers to their curiosities by asking open-ended questions that spark conversation and critical thinking. Foster a culture of inquiry and curiosity by encouraging children to wonder, speculate, and investigate.

3. **Promote Outdoor Play:** Encourage outdoor play and exploration as a means of fostering curiosity and

creativity. Provide opportunities for children to explore natural environments, engage in unstructured play, and discover the wonders of the world around them.

4. **Support Diverse Interests:** Respect and support children's diverse interests and passions, even if they may differ from your own. Encourage them to pursue activities and hobbies that ignite their curiosity and bring them joy, and provide resources and support to help them explore their interests further.

5. **Encourage Risk-Taking in Learning:** Foster a culture of experimentation and risk-taking in learning by creating a safe space where children feel comfortable trying new things and making mistakes. Encourage them to embrace challenges, take initiative, and learn from both successes and failures.

6. **Provide Opportunities for Hands-On Learning:** Offer hands-on learning experiences that allow children to actively engage with materials, manipulate objects, and experiment with different concepts and ideas. Provide opportunities for exploration, discovery, and problem-solving that encourage children to think creatively and critically.

By striking a balance between safety and opportunities for growth and encouraging curiosity and exploration, you help children develop the confidence, resilience, and critical thinking skills needed to navigate the complexities of the world around them. Your support and guidance play a crucial role in fostering a sense of wonder and curiosity in children and empowering them to embrace new experiences and challenges with enthusiasm and courage.

Cultivating Social Skills and Empathy

As a caregiver or educator, cultivating social skills and empathy in children is essential for their personal and interpersonal development. By teaching cooperation and collaboration and fostering empathy and understanding of others, you empower children to build meaningful relationships, communicate effectively, and navigate social interactions with kindness and compassion. In this section, we will explore practical strategies to promote social skills and empathy in the children under your care.

Teaching Cooperation and Collaboration

1. **Promote Teamwork:** Encourage children to work together towards common goals and objectives by promoting teamwork and collaboration.

Provide opportunities for group activities, projects, and games that require cooperation and collective problem-solving.

2. **Model Cooperative Behavior:** Be a positive role model for cooperation and collaboration by demonstrating respectful communication, compromise, and teamwork in your interactions with others. Highlight the importance of working together towards shared goals and celebrating collective achievements.

3. **Assign Group Tasks:** Assign group tasks or projects that require children to collaborate and contribute their unique strengths and perspectives. Encourage them to delegate responsibilities, communicate effectively, and support one another in achieving shared objectives.

4. **Encourage Active Listening:** Teach children the importance of active

listening in fostering cooperation and collaboration. Encourage them to listen attentively to others' ideas, opinions, and perspectives, and to express their thoughts and feelings respectfully and assertively.

5. **Resolve Conflict Constructively:** Help children develop conflict resolution skills by teaching them constructive ways to address disagreements and conflicts that may arise during group activities. Encourage them to communicate openly, listen to each other's viewpoints, and work towards mutually satisfactory solutions.

6. **Celebrate Team Success:** Celebrate the success of collaborative efforts and teamwork by acknowledging and praising the contributions of each team member. Highlight the strengths and achievements of the group as a whole, reinforcing the value of cooperation and collaboration in achieving shared goals.

Developing Empathy and Understanding of Others

1.   **Promote   Perspective-Taking:** Encourage children to consider things from others' perspectives by asking questions such as "How do you think they feel?" or "Guess in your mind what they are experiencing?" Encourage them to empathize with others' emotions and experiences to develop a deeper understanding and appreciation of their feelings.

2. **Model Empathetic Behavior:** Model empathetic behavior by demonstrating kindness, compassion, and empathy in your interactions with others. Show children how to recognize and respond to others' emotions with empathy and understanding, and encourage them to follow your example.

3. **Practice Active Listening:** Teach children the importance of active

listening in developing empathy and understanding. Encourage them to listen attentively to others' thoughts, feelings, and experiences without judgment or interruption, and to validate their emotions and perspectives.

4. **Encourage Perspective-Sharing:** Create opportunities for children to share their thoughts, feelings, and experiences with others, and to listen to and learn from the perspectives of their peers. Encourage open and honest communication, and foster a culture of empathy and understanding within the group.

5. **Promote Empathetic Actions:** Encourage children to take empathetic actions towards others by demonstrating kindness, compassion, and consideration in their interactions. Encourage them to offer support, assistance, and encouragement to those in need, and to stand up for others

who may be experiencing hardship or adversity.

6. **Discuss Diversity and Inclusion:** Facilitate discussions about diversity, inclusion, and social justice to help children develop empathy and understanding towards people from different backgrounds, cultures, and perspectives. Encourage them to embrace diversity and celebrate the unique qualities and contributions of individuals from all walks of life.

By teaching cooperation and collaboration and fostering empathy and understanding of others, you help children develop essential social skills and emotional intelligence that will serve them well throughout their lives. Your guidance and support play a crucial role in nurturing their ability to build positive relationships, communicate effectively, and navigate the complexities of the social world with kindness, compassion, and empathy.

Addressing Challenges and Adversity

Navigating challenges and adversity is an inevitable part of life, and as a caregiver or educator, supporting children through tough times and building resilience in the face of adversity is essential for their well-being and growth. By providing guidance, encouragement, and resources, you empower children to overcome obstacles, develop coping skills, and emerge stronger and more resilient. In this section, we will explore practical strategies to address challenges and adversity in the children under your care.

Supporting Children Through Tough Times

1. **Create a Safe and Supportive Environment:** Foster a safe and supportive environment where children

feel comfortable expressing their thoughts, feelings, and concerns. Let them know that you are there to listen, support, and validate their experiences without judgment or criticism.

2. **Be Present and Available:** Make yourself available to children during tough times by being present, attentive, and responsive to their needs. Take the time to check in with them regularly, ask how they are feeling, and offer your support and reassurance.

3. **Validate Their Feelings:** Validate children's feelings and experiences by acknowledging and accepting their emotions without judgment. Let them know that it's okay to feel sad, angry, or scared, and reassure them that you are there to support them through whatever they may be going through.

4. **Encourage Open Communication:** Encourage open communication by

creating opportunities for children to express themselves and share their thoughts and feelings. Be a compassionate listener, and provide a safe space for them to talk about their worries, fears, and struggles.

5. **Offer Practical Support:** Offer practical support to help children cope with tough times, such as providing resources, guidance, or referrals to additional support services if needed. Help them identify healthy coping strategies and self-care practices to manage stress and build resilience.

6. **Model Healthy Coping Behaviors:** Be a positive role model for healthy coping behaviors by demonstrating resilience, optimism, and effective problem-solving skills in your own life. Show children how to navigate challenges with grace and strength, and emphasize the importance of self-care and seeking support when needed.

Building Resilience in the Face of Adversity

1. **Promote a Growth Mindset:** Foster a growth mindset in children by emphasizing the importance of effort, perseverance, and learning from mistakes. Encourage them to view challenges as opportunities for growth and learning, rather than obstacles to be feared or avoided.

2. **Encourage Problem-Solving Skills:** Teach children problem-solving skills to help them navigate challenges and adversity effectively. Encourage them to break problems down into smaller, manageable steps, brainstorm possible solutions, and evaluate the consequences of their actions.

3. **Develop Coping Strategies:** Help children develop healthy coping strategies to manage stress and adversity. Teach them relaxation

techniques such as deep breathing or mindfulness, encourage physical activity and creative expression, and provide opportunities for them to engage in activities that bring them joy and comfort.

4. **Build Social Support Networks:** Encourage children to build strong social support networks by fostering positive relationships with family, friends, teachers, and other trusted adults. Teach them how to seek support when needed, and encourage them to offer support to others in return.

5. **Promote Resilient Thinking Patterns:** Help children develop resilient thinking patterns by challenging negative thoughts and beliefs and replacing them with more positive and empowering ones. Encourage them to focus on their strengths and past successes, and remind them of their

ability to overcome challenges and adversity.

6. **Celebrate Resilience:** Celebrate children's resilience and perseverance in the face of adversity by acknowledging their efforts and achievements. Highlight their strengths, resilience, and growth, and reinforce their belief in their ability to overcome challenges and thrive.

By supporting children through tough times and building resilience in the face of adversity, you empower them to navigate life's challenges with confidence, strength, and resilience. Your guidance, support, and encouragement play a crucial role in helping children develop the skills, attitudes, and mindset necessary to overcome obstacles and emerge stronger and more resilient than ever before.

Celebrating Successes and Progress

Celebrating successes and progress is vital for children's motivation, self-esteem, and overall well-being. As a caregiver or educator, recognizing and celebrating achievements and reinforcing positive behavior and effort are essential practices that help children feel valued, motivated, and confident in their abilities. In this section, we will explore practical strategies to celebrate successes and progress in the children under your care.

Recognizing and Celebrating Achievements

1. **Acknowledge Small Wins:** Celebrate even the smallest accomplishments and milestones to reinforce children's efforts and progress. Whether it's completing a task, mastering a new skill, or demonstrating

positive behavior, take the time to acknowledge and praise their achievements.

2. **Create Milestone Markers:** Set up milestone markers or visual representations of progress, such as charts, graphs, or stickers, to track children's accomplishments over time. Celebrate reaching each milestone with a special reward or recognition to motivate continued effort and progress.

3. **Hold Recognition Ceremonies:** Organize recognition ceremonies or events to honor children's achievements and milestones publicly. Invite family members, friends, or peers to join in the celebration and share in their accomplishments, making them feel proud and supported.

4. **Personalized Recognition:** Personalize recognition and celebration of each child's interests, preferences,

and strengths. Tailor rewards and incentives to align with their individual goals and aspirations, showing that you value and appreciate their unique contributions and achievements.

5. **Encourage Peer Recognition:** Foster a culture of peer recognition by encouraging children to celebrate each other's successes and accomplishments. Provide opportunities for them to offer compliments, praise, and encouragement to their peers, reinforcing positive behavior and building a supportive community.

6. **Celebrate Effort, Not Just Outcome:** Focus on celebrating effort and progress rather than just the outcome. Emphasize the importance of hard work, perseverance, and resilience in achieving success, and praise children for their dedication and commitment to reaching their goals.

Reinforcing Positive Behavior and Effort

1. **Use Positive Reinforcement:** Reinforce positive behavior and effort with praise, encouragement, and rewards to motivate continued growth and progress. Acknowledge and celebrate instances of kindness, generosity, perseverance, and other positive behaviors to reinforce their importance.

2. **Offer Specific Feedback:** Provide specific and meaningful feedback that highlights the connection between children's actions and the positive outcomes they achieve. Recognize the specific behaviors or efforts that lead to success and praise them for their contributions.

3. **Set Clear Expectations:** Set clear expectations for behavior and effort and communicate them consistently to children. Help them understand what is

expected of them and why it's important, and provide guidance and support to help them meet those expectations.

4. **Use Incentives and Rewards:** Offer incentives and rewards to reinforce positive behavior and effort and motivate children to continue making progress towards their goals. Use a variety of rewards, such as verbal praise, privileges, stickers, or tokens, to keep children engaged and motivated.

5. **Encourage Self-Reflection:** Encourage children to reflect on their behavior and effort and recognize the connection between their actions and the outcomes they achieve. Help them identify areas for improvement and set goals for continued growth and development.

6. **Model Positive Behavior:** Be a positive role model for behavior and effort by demonstrating kindness,

perseverance, and a positive attitude in your interactions with children. Show them the importance of taking responsibility for their actions and making an effort to improve themselves.

By recognizing and celebrating achievements and reinforcing positive behavior and effort, you help children feel valued, motivated, and confident in their abilities. Your encouragement and support play a crucial role in fostering a positive and nurturing environment where children feel empowered to reach their full potential and celebrate their successes along the way.

Conclusion

As you conclude your journey in exploring how to build confidence in kids, it's essential to reflect on the key points discussed throughout this book and consider how you can apply them to support the children in your care. From understanding the importance of confidence to cultivating social skills and resilience, you've gained valuable insights and practical strategies to empower children to thrive in today's world. In this final section, we'll summarize the key points covered and offer some final thoughts and encouragement to inspire you on your continued journey of nurturing confidence in children.

Summarizing Key Points

Throughout this book, you've learned:

- The importance of confidence in children's overall development and well-being.
- How to define confidence and its components, as well as the benefits of building confidence in kids.
- Common obstacles children face in developing confidence and the external factors that impact their confidence.
- Strategies for creating a supportive environment at home, nurturing self-esteem, and fostering positive self-image.
- Effective communication techniques to communicate positively with children and encourage openness and expressiveness.
- The importance of encouraging independence and resilience in decision-making and teaching coping skills.
- Promoting a growth mindset and goal setting to empower children to embrace challenges and achieve their aspirations.

- Strategies for embracing failure as a natural part of learning and encouraging reflection and adaptation.
- Cultivating healthy risk-taking and exploration by balancing safety with opportunities for growth and encouraging curiosity.
- Developing social skills and empathy through teaching cooperation, collaboration, and empathy.
- Addressing challenges and adversity by supporting children through tough times and building resilience.
- Celebrating successes and progress by recognizing achievements, and reinforcing positive behavior, and effort.

Final Thoughts and Encouragement

As you continue on your journey of supporting children in building confidence, remember that every child is unique and may require different approaches and strategies. Be patient, flexible, and compassionate in your interactions with children, and always prioritize their well-being and growth.

Embrace the role of a positive role model, demonstrating confidence, resilience, and empathy in your actions and attitudes. Your words and behaviors have a powerful impact on children's development and self-perception, so strive to lead by example and inspire them to reach their full potential.

Celebrate the progress and successes of the children in your care, no matter how small, and encourage them to celebrate their achievements as well. By fostering a culture of positivity, support, and encouragement, you create an environment where children feel valued, motivated, and empowered to pursue their dreams and aspirations.

Remember that building confidence in children is an ongoing process that requires patience, dedication, and commitment. Be willing to adapt and evolve your strategies as you learn and grow alongside the children in your care, and never underestimate the profound impact you can have on their lives.

As you embark on this journey, know that you are making a difference in the lives of the children you touch, helping them develop the confidence and resilience they need to succeed in school, relationships, and life. Your efforts are invaluable, and your dedication to nurturing confidence in children is truly commendable.

With perseverance, empathy, and a steadfast commitment to supporting children's growth and development, you can help shape a brighter future for generations to come. Thank you for your dedication and passion in building confidence in kids.